Forged in the Stars

Celine McGlynn

For Eddi

A gift to meet you

Celine
Lamotton 9/8/12.

SUMMER PALACE PRESS

First published in 2011 by

Summer Palace Press
Cladnageeragh, Kilbeg, Kilcar, County Donegal, Ireland
and
31 Stranmillis Park, Belfast BT9 5AU

in association with
Donegal County Council

Printed by Nicholson & Bass Ltd.

A catalogue record for this book is available from the British Library

ISBN 978-0-905989-38-6

FSC
Mixed Sources
Product group from well-managed
forests, controlled sources and
recycled wood or fibre
Cert no. SGS-COC-005221
www.fsc.org
© 1996 Forest Stewardship Council

This book is printed on elemental chlorine-free paper

for Bartley

Acknowledgments

Some of the poems in this book have previously appeared in: *Beyond the Rubicon* (Covehill Press 1999); *Brass on Bronze* (Errigal Press 2005); *Eleven Ways to Kiss the Ground* (Errigal Writers CD); *Poetry Ireland Review* (Issue 46 and Issue 50) and *Women's Work* (VII).

Biographical Note

Celine McGlynn is editor of the long-established newspaper, the *Finn Valley Voice*. As a visual artist she has exhibited widely. She is the editor of *The Best of William Allingham* and *Sarah Leech, the Ulster-Scots poetess of Raphoe, Co. Donegal*, both of whom have been unjustly neglected as writers. A founder member of the Errigal Writers, her work has appeared in both of the group's anthologies – *Beyond the Rubicon* and *Brass on Bronze*, and their CD, *Eleven Ways to Kiss the Ground*, as well as in various poetry magazines.

CONTENTS

Blue July

for Amy Winehouse

I start this day without you,
the first day of summer
you'll never see.
I dream that you are older
and walking by a river.
The music reaches you
but never gets to me.

I start this day without you,
this birthday without you.
Did you hear Edith sing?
Did she find your heart,
tear it out, let it soar?

I dream that you are running
in a storm in Monticello.
The trees crash around you,
your face is drenched with rain.
The road becomes a river
takes the music with it.
Are you going home?
Is the road back very long?

I dream that you are falling
with a man who holds your hand.
The mist comes down, covers him,
his face is in the space between.
You look into his eyes
and you are lost again.

He feeds on your sorrow,
it fills his heart and brain.
Then he gifts it back to you,
opens all your wounds again.

I see you at a party
on a summer night,
I see your friends,
fear for them,
for risks I'll never take,
for songs I'll never sing.
But they become like rainbows
arched across the sky,
vanish into notes,
sing this blue July.

The Starry Night

after Van Gogh

He knows the sky because he looks
at the vast blue and sees his heart,
looks into his own eyes.
Hears the music that is played
when his brush touches the canvas,
a burning cypress flames up and up.
He might tell Theo that the quiet village
becomes his starry sky every night.
The sleeping people leave
their beds and take to the blue hills,
gather shimmering flowers for their hair,
cover their bodies in moonlight.
He sees his pulsing sky whorl a radiant moon,
draw everyone to it, through a church
spire that holds the centre,
keeps it, until dawn breaks.

Birthday Card

She asked me to help
her choose a card for
her daughter's birthday.
I haven't my glasses with me.

Together we look through
the offerings on display.
She picks pink flowers
for 'A Special Daughter.'

Maybe you would
write it for me.
Put 'Love, Mum and Dad' on it
'God Bless and Happy Birthday.'

Maggie

My grandmother was a smile
in a halo of Woodbine.
A room where I dared
to believe in something more.
A song of days spent cleaning
carpets in the Bán Field.
A night to hold
the laughter of summer,
days spent in secret conversation.
A bed dressed in white cotton.
She was the light beside the fire
and she burned brighter.

Scratch Heaven

He was sitting in a car
outside the paper shop.
I knew he was looking
at a scratch card.
His right shoulder moved
over and back
quivering
revealing stars.

Bird

My eye is caught by a flying bird
as they gather around the coffin bed.
I keep a safe distance, watch detached
as they hum the prayers, weep their goodbyes.
The bird returns, swoops low and high again,
glories in the open uncharted space.
I remember the veins drained of blood,
swelled with the fluid of light.
The prayers have wrung themselves out;
I leave them alone to the last farewell.
I want to feel clean, cold air fill my lungs,
discover the bird's final turn.
Watch as the coffin is carried from the house,
see it rest in the back of a long black hearse.

St Thérèse

Early morning market town
outside the cathedral.
People talk in an ordinary way
as they go inside holding roses.
The queue moves slowly
to the glass dome, a cover
for her remains.
The saint looks down
at kisses on her bones.

Young men in work clothes
from building sites,
women with small children,
people in wheelchairs,
pushchairs and families
all carry roses,
white, red, yellow, peach.
A man carries a careless
bunch, upside down.
You can leave the flowers
or take them with you
into the day where
flower sellers call out:
One euro each, the roses.

Currently Unemployed

The insurance form arrives
and asks the usual questions:
Do you own your own home?
Is it semi-detached or detached?
What sector do you work in
and your spouse too?

The spouse works from dawn until dark,
cooking, cleaning, baking, mending,
has a part time job,
sews, sculpts, writes too,
and he asks:
Will I write 'currently unemployed' for you?

Brown Hair Dancing

Late again.
She said she would be here
at six o'clock.
It is half past seven.

Go in the direction
I hope she'll come from,
think of things to say.
Decide on punishments –
no discos,
no friends to stay.

Watch for her
around every bend,
tightness in my chest.

Then I see
brown hair dancing,
long limbs walking,
the closest I get to being free.

Little Girl

She alights
from a green
minibus.

With head
slightly bent
she floats
to the ground
after her first
day at school.

In a red coat
she is bright
she is distant.

Reporter

Delete the line in the story
I wrote that said:
Annie McIntyre, mother
of seventeen and wife
of Willie Duncan
who was her neighbour, not her husband.
Delete the frantic attempt
to cross out the wrong name
in thousands of newspapers
on shelves in shops waiting to be bought.
Delete the lunacy of working all night long.
Delete the deadlines and the story lines
that did not need to be written,
delete every word that was rushed
or forced or just used to fill a space.
Keep the words that attempted truth
and something of grace.
For the women in the courts
who begged me not to write
their children's shame.
The trembling backs of boys who swear
to tell the truth, the whole truth
and promise never to do it again.

Girls

He gave us a lift
in his car,
my three daughters
and me.

Are they all yours?
he said.
Three brown-eyed children
look at me.

They're all girls,
he said.
I agree.
Ah well, said he.

Custard

How we laughed in bed
together, you and I.
Words like 'custard'
made us scream.
Dissect the word,
'cus' – hilarious,
'tard' – so funny it hurts.
The imaginary line
down the middle
of our single bed
guarded our separateness,
kept us whole.
You begged for songs,
sing me another one.
I sang every song I knew.

Castlefin

My country tastes of brambles
and smells of honeysuckle and after-rain.
The mist covers her morning,
lifts to reveal a shy rose deep in a hedge.
Hers is the silence of long shadows,
the dancing of a withered leaf.
Hers the stillness of a frosty morning,
a crisp kiss at the throat of the day.

She is Yvonne who can take a day
that was going nowhere and give it back.
She is Paddy forever young and Nuala
on a bicycle flowing a river of auburn hair.
She is Rita, who takes us to graves
in Monellan where the Delaps lie,
their dogs buried at their feet.
She is Mary cooling milk at dawn.
She is Gerry who sees so much.
And Tommy stacking corn.

She is a field of straggling gooseberry
bushes, hedged with lilac blossom,
a many-roomed tree house,
an orchard of pear, apple and plum.
She is Debbie, the hurricane
who ripped out the roots.
She is the place on the road back
from my last day in 5th class,
where the unfamiliar ache of something
unknown has no words to articulate
that I want to stay at home.

Beat

She found her mother
in the attic with the rope.

She cut the rope into pieces
before she called for help.

He was in a band, a nice man
who had other women.

Mantilla

for my mother

Did you catch
sight of yourself
as you fixed
the mantilla
on that dark
glossy head
with the flashes
of red?
Did you, when
you tiptoed silently
into the pew,
remember sitting
on the rocks
laughing –
your head
thrown back,
the wind
and the sun
casting lots
to be first
to play
with your hair?

Scent

I must get ready for the wake,
all those people coming
for the last goodbye.
I need a new hoover,

an electric kettle and a cooker.
I'll never manage the range
now she's gone.
Where would I get a hoover?

I'll get the cooker and kettle.
Why did she leave me
with all this bother?
She's gone and I'm not well at all

and I have to buy all these things
and food on top of that.
They will all want sandwiches,
biscuits and cigarettes.

The people who sit up
will have to get drink.
Who can I get to buy the things?
I don't want to go and get them.

She planted roses
when we got married.
Remember the scent of flowers
on her clothes.

She's so still.
Won't complain now about
not having this, not having that.
Always wanted to go on holiday.

I don't want to go into the house.
I want her in it.
There is no point in anything
now that she is gone.

The Reek

We do not know what lies ahead.
Laughter and pilgrim talk leads us on.
It rises before us, bathed in the sun.
We have a day, we have the Reek.

The pilgrim who stops to chat is local,
knows how to come down without falling –
You never dig your heel in, use the front of your foot,
sideways is safer coming down a mountain.

I can feel my breath. Another step on soft grass after rock.
The mountain stream sings me a travelling song, a passing praise.
Your voice dances on my ear. Your plans are our progress.
Steady companions, we leave no trace.

We stop and breathe in Mayo,
drink water and taste blue-cool on our tongues,
marvel at our little world, leave it behind.
There's no room for cares today, just one step, no time.

Why did Patrick choose this hill and not another?
Did he long for this summit where he could stop and pray,
touch the gate at the highest point,
see the islands in the bay?

No Victory

Whatever we are, it is not this
and when we die, no warm hand
to clasp in greeting.
No smile to lift the day,
distant sound of piper,
lambs munching grass,
seagull-proud breast,
sunlight stream or daylight
creeping into morning,
cool floor underfoot,
sound of you breaking shells
of crab claws fresh from the sea,
quiet days to make me strong again,
hum of a ferry engine,
peach rose on the path,
May bluebells in Drumboe,
victory sip from the cup.
No mother
no father
no son
no daughter.

Tears

I asked the young girl
Do you cry at the sad
parts in books?
No, she said.
Tears fill my eyes
but they don't fall down.

Franz Kafka

I find my way to the place
of his memory in Prague.
I learn he was shy, unsure.
I meet him too late now to know
There is a destination
The road is hesitation
The cage is looking for a bird.
This poem is a prayer
I have not begun to say
with any conviction.
So much will be left undone.
The body is only a beautiful illusion.

Pound Street

The man didn't know
the stones from our first home
were in his digger bucket.

He didn't know that these stones
had sheltered our promise
to be, always.

He could not see us in our twenties
walking up the narrow stairs to
our one-room flat with its
tiny bedroom and windows to
our first main road.

He could not hear us laughing
when our landlord told us we
were mad to get married.

He did not see your hand
cup my face when we knew
our first child would be born.

He was a man at work
with stones and clay.

Doors

She didn't always let people in
when they came to her door.

You said you worried that she stayed
out of sight when you called.

I asked you if it were me
who could not let you in

would you care enough
to find out why.

Feet

My father's feet
marble on a cushion
the bones
under the skin
still.

The Goldsmith

I looked for a memory of her,
went through drawers where she
kept the sheets and bedclothes,
the white lace especially for wakes.
She stood at so many bedsides,
said so many goodbyes.

A rosary said her name.
I did not touch it.
The aprons were true.
The blue one with the red flowers.
She remembers herself, a child,
in a dress with the same pattern,
who looked at her mother's face for the last time
as she boarded a train that took her to a hospital –
her last home.
Her telephone book was there,
with its rows of neat names followed by numbers.
My name was written there.

Then I found it, the box, pink and gold
with two gold rings.
Not her wedding ring but a special one,
a ring from someone she loved
who lived where earth and sky,
tree and stone made a place to grow.
And the other ring with a scar
where the goldsmith
added a length to make it fit.

Risk

It was a risk to let you take me down the slope
through virgin snow.
The small sleigh flew on fragile wooden slats.
Your arms around my waist the only security
in a world that was flashing by.
We left lifetimes in our wake,
blazed a trail through a frozen lake.
Sometimes now when I am afraid to take a risk,
settling for less,
I feel a cold rush of wind and stifled breath.

Luck's a Funny Thing

Good luck come and bad luck go
and luck's a funny thing – Anne Dolan

The fortune teller said for twenty euro
she would blow away the sadness
that surrounds my family and me.
See her draw in the air of Ballybofey,
fill her lungs to capacity and blow away
the uncertainty about how to be a mother
afraid of doing the wrong thing, of causing harm.
And the harm.

Blow away the pot of beef bourguignon
that fell on Sarah.
Blow away the boiling kettle
on the bathroom floor that Maeve
crawled into on her first birthday.

Blow Nuala away from the car
that hit her on Navenney Street
when she ran across to see the new Centra shop.
Hold her rag-doll body as it fell through the air
to hit the bonnet, then the ground.
Bring back the relief of her unmarked form
in a white hospital gown.

Blow away all their pain.
Blow away the months without laughter
while we waited for the scars to heal
but not the ripple of it as it bubbled
from my belly,
a new sensation,
forgotten for so long.

Going Solo

You were the only one from the class
on the sideline in your school uniform
while everyone else wore the jersey.
Your friends said it wasn't fair,
one girl shrugged her shoulders,
made a solo run down the pitch.
You had prepared so well.
Your boots splayed in front of the fire
the night before.
The skin hardened,
became tough.

Light

Ordinary things
made sacred with the light.
How it would fall on a page
gentle as I read.
How precious now the apples, how red.
The oranges, the oranges.
And his form, the strength of it,
how it was part of the day.
Their faces, the brown eyes,
the way it shone on their heads,
the shape of them.
The evening,
how it loved the mountain,
was reluctant to leave,
went so easy,
like a falling prayer.

Vessel

Look at it in all
its unlovely loveliness.
The cracks, dull colour, uneven
edges. The flaking, falling apart,
falling to nothingness;
look at it –
is that light shining through?

I have waited for you
since time began.
My being forged in the stars
longed for your touch.
How you moulded me,
strong, yet delicate.
Capable of holding
all that sustains,
all that blesses.

Fill me with water,
pour it on rich, soft soil.
Let me show you joy;
for your touch has redeemed me,
brought me home.

Old Dances, New Places

To Ellis Island they carried handmade things,
embroidered cloths, beaded wedding shoes,
to take a step into the New World.

They waited in lines to hear a new name being called,
they watched as kin were marked with chalk,
were singled out for more questions.

They walked on different stairs,
to East, to West, to wait.

See them run with arms outstretched
to relatives waiting at the Kissing Post.

Trevi

In Rome, we turn a corner.
There it is in gleaming white stone.
Horses, heralds and angels
bow to rushing water.
Fountains gush and faces
take in the wonder of Trevi.

Did a God carve that head?
That horse, did he gallop
at full speed, a rider on his back
through sparkling blue waters?
That couple, the middle-aged couple;
the girl and boy, their backs
to the fountain, throwing coins.
Did they wish for anything real?

My father's hands and feet
were beautiful, like the hands
of the guardians of Trevi,
the God of the sea and his sons.

His presence the loud
rushing water of the fountain.
I was cowed by his wild rages,
ached for his blessing.
His absence, a wound on the heart;
like going back to Rome;
turning that corner to find it
empty of the miracle of stone.

Antiques

The crucified Christ
is the centrepiece
of a window display
in an antique shop
in Dublin,

flanked by St Patrick
and a candelabra with
price tags that
would not appeal
to the poor or the spirit.

Unlit church candles,
an empty tabernacle,
a dusty chalice,
stripped of reverence.

Who will buy this religion?
Who will mourn the Christ?

The Watcher

If I could find a key
to reveal
lost depths of your
child heart, I would
hold it for a long long
time; warm it in my
hand and ask you: *Do you*
wish to remember innocence
and where did wonder go?
What freedom was it
that did not know
its name and when exactly
the watcher came?

Outlaw

Here is the wild woman.
Here is the deep guttural
roar passed through pain.

She is the mountain hag
who leaves a perfect footprint
on the earth, her kingdom.

Her dress
is the crushed blue silk
of the Downings sea.

She eats wild berries
that stain her hands, her skin.
She makes her home in a cave.

Was she once a child
waking up,
holding her breath?

Did she sit on the branch
of an apple tree and pray
until there was nothing left?

Longing to embrace the wild woman,
look into her bog-pool eyes,
listen to the cockcrow of her mornings?

Not infrequently

He said to her:
*I think about you
and not infrequently
maybe five or six
times a week.
Sometimes only for
a second
and sometimes longer.*

More Than Blue

The blue of
remembered
summer skies
still shines from my
mother's blue blue eyes.

Lost in the warm
blue ocean of her love
that is more than love
and more than blue.

All else pales beside
the blue blue brightness
of her eyes.

Harvest

At last, a harvest
of purple plums
from the sapling planted
long ago.

It took years to yield anything.
Tiny bare branches
leafed every year,
barren.

And then one late August,
a perfect purple plum,
another and another.

Until we taste
in the kitchen
from bowls spilling over,
sweet, ripe, golden flesh.

Island

They are a community
in the old way,
hold the traditions,
keep them for another generation.
Time stands still,
it hardly matters at all.
What more do you need
but the song of the sea?

The other side,
the rich sea sold,
fishing boats empty,
whiskey-coloured nights,
aimless days,
a long queue at the surgery,
sons and daughters
gone to far-away places.

Tea

He loved his tea hot and strong,
made with real leaves.
Two spoonfuls in a scalded mug
filled with boiling water.
A trace of milk faded the red.

The comfort of the clink
of mug on saucer,
the heat on palm cradle,
veins warmed.
Sipped slowly,
draining to an ancient
scarred landscape.

First Love

She has tried for days
to tell me.
I know by the way
she stands too close
with nothing to say.

She looks at me
and smiles too bright,
What is it, dote?
It's nothing, I'm alright.

A walk in the woods.
At last she speaks:
I have a boyfriend, Mammy.
He has pale blue eyes,
the loveliest smile.
And he is cracked about me.

Not Mustard

I like the hand-painted silk scarves
I find here.
The intensity of the colour,
turquoise jewel brightness,
vibrant red.

A little bird comes in.
I still don't know the names of birds.
The head is blue and the breast is orange.

The girl at the next table drinks golden tea.
She wears yellow, dark, not mustard.

Shadow

We were friends,
aware of each other
through all the days.
We raced as one,
noted the lengthening,
the shortening.
Together,
where there was light
we made shadow
animals, dogs,
cats, foxes,
and all manner of birds
with long-arm necks.
And strange beasts
with no names.
I found, in you, comfort,
no need for words.

Mother

What was your mother's name?
He can remember
waiting for her on the road
to come back from the town.
He can remember the smell of her
as she kissed him goodnight.
He can remember
bowls of hot porridge
and pancakes handed out
the moment they were cooked.
He can see her face
the day he left to go to England.
He can remember her last breath,
the dull sound of her coffin
as they lowered it down
all those years ago.
Now he sits, head in his hands,
searching for her name.

Prayer

Andrea Bocelli's voice in the car
finds some forgotten tenderness in me,
makes me forget who I am,
what I do, where I am going.
His longing becomes my own.

Listening to him,
the school children on the footpath
are beautiful, their moving bodies,
the joints beneath the skin,
muscles hold them as they
fall forward,
forever falling.

Home

Like sand he falls through
the hour glass of my life.
He softens the edges,
touches me so easily
as if we are one body.
Soft breath from between
his parted lips fuses
air around my face.
When he kisses,
it is coming home.

Labyrinth

I've got you now.
Never mind the Minotaur.
You think he has power
taking the blood of seven boys and girls.

When you see the Minotaur
you find a truth,
but I take the truth.
I leave confusion in its place.

I am a game
where you are blind,
falling, falling, falling
out of space.

The Spirit of the Dance

Standing face to face
for the hand jive.
Hold hands.
The music starts, the twirl
and anti-twirl of bodies become
a whirlpool older than an eye
seeing what it wants,
fresh as a sheet on the line.

You have the music in you,
the spirit of the dance.
It isn't strength though it helps,
it isn't technique when two
are seamless – a lonely arc
longing to know itself.
It is just so easy to trust
your hand to spin me
weightless through aeons
straight to now.

When Liam Plays Guitar

He doesn't play to you,
the music he takes
is for himself, a lifeline
he keeps throwing
from hands that know
how to dance.

The Dancer
for Anne

You have the sea in you,
know its deep secret,
when we are children
on Narin strand.

The rhythm of dance
strong in you.
The ocean
an echo in you.

We walk into the sea,
walk and walk
deeper and deeper.

There is no going back,
the sea draws our bodies,
laughs at our little waving hands.
But you
know the pause,
know exactly
when to pull us
back to stinging sand.

Other Things

You show me the photograph
of your grandchild,
an angel in christening white.

You are alive with wonder,
grateful for the gift she brings.

We often meet in the town
and you barely say *hello*.

But today
you do all the talking – her smiles,
her mum, her dad, the way
she closes her eyes.

Your eyes are bright with hope
and sometimes glance at the window.

Then he appears,
the one you have been waiting for.
He sees you and says:
Are you deaf with every other effin thing.

The Resting Stone

He carried his father
to the workhouse
in a creel.

His father said:
Son, rest at that big stone.
Why, father?
Son, I rested at that stone
when I carried my father
to the workhouse.